Gardens of Gravel and Sand

Leonard Koren

Stone Bridge Press
Berkeley, California

Many thanks to the following people for their invaluable assistance during the preparation of this book: Pamela Burton, Peter Goodman, Ron Herman, Taishi Hirokawa, the staff at Horiuchi Color (Kyoto), Henry Kaiser, Marc P. Keane, the staff at Labo Take (Tokyo), Henry Mittwer, Takahiro Naka, Shiro Nakane, Greg Reeder, D. M. Roth, David A. Slawson, Naoko Terazaki, and especially Gretchen Mittwer and Ziggie Y. Kato.

Published by Stone Bridge Press, P.O. Box 8208, Berkeley, CA 94707, USA

Photography and book design by the author: leonardkoren.com

Printed in the United States of America

ISBN 1-880656-43-4

Contents

No rocks

All the photographs in this book, various configurations and treatments of gravel and sand, were taken during May 1999 in Kyoto, Japan.[1] Many of the photographs were shot at formal "dry landscape"—*kare-san-sui*—gardens located on the grounds of Zen Buddhist temples or former samurai villas now under Zen Buddhist caretaking.[2] Others were documented at either non-Zen Buddhist temples or Shinto shrines. None of the photographs, however, is intended to be visually descriptive of the particular place *in toto* where it was taken. The non-specificity of the locations—almost as if the photographs could have been taken anyplace—is intended to limit distraction from our subject matter: gardens of gravel and sand.[3]

The inclusion of trees and shrubs, which are often seen just adjacent to the gravel or sand, was also avoided in the picture taking whenever possible. Plant materials represent a dynamic of Nature wherein things grow effortlessly of their own accord.[4] The making of gardens of gravel and sand, conversely, represents a conscious attempt to *not* let Nature blithely proceed as it will. A well-maintained gravel or sand garden demands constant opposition to Nature's tendencies with regular cleaning, weeding, raking, and/or re-forming.

Finally, rocks, too, were avoided, although often this was not possible. Rocks are the "celebrity" features of many Japanese gardens. They are prominently positioned everywhere. They are fawned over and sometimes even given individual names. Hence the adoring English sobriquet, "Japanese rock garden." But these same cherished rocks also cause many people to overlook the "lowly" gravel and sand—or to dismiss it as mere background to the rocks' exalted "figure" status.[5]

By severely reducing these extraneous and/or antagonistic visual and conceptual elements, what have we lost? We've thrown away predictable images of idealized Japanese gardens. We've jettisoned obsessive emphasis on "profound connoisseurship," "extraordinary sensitivity," or highly specialized skill in garden design and construction. And we've obliterated at least 1,500 years of Chinese and Japanese garden history, hazy at best, virtually none of which is devoted to the gravel and sand anyway.[6]

On the other hand, by focusing only on the gravel and sand, we've retained clear and irrefutable evidence of a keen and persistent human intelligence at play. We've honed in on an unusual, subtle, and often whimsical sense of visual poetry. And, in paring down solely to the gravel and sand, we've gained a simple vehicle to highlight ironic perspectives in a way that venerable place, luxuriant vegetation, and curious rocks could never do.

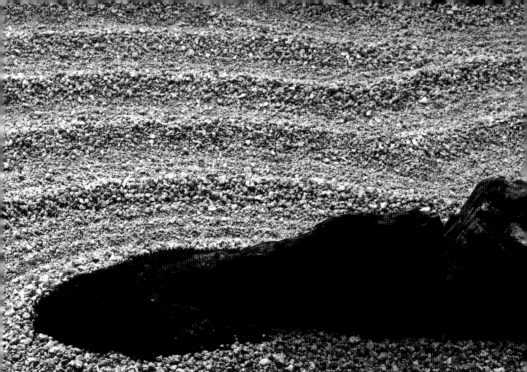

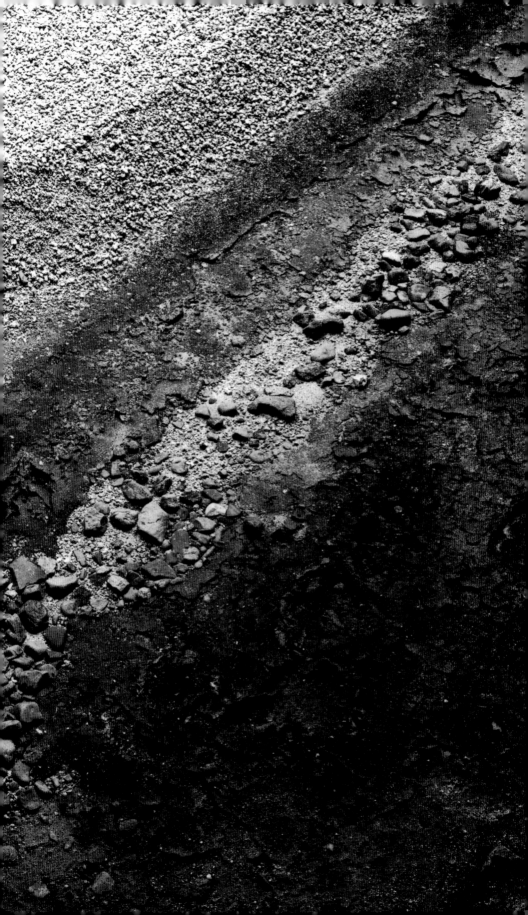

Not Zen

A part of our perverse attraction to the use of gravel or sand in the construction of *anything* is the Sisyphean absurdity of such endeavors. Tentativeness, ephemerality, and instability are the qualities we commonly associate with such building materials. The notion of intentionally working in gravel or sand—especially sand—is virtually metaphoric for attempting something pointedly trivial or futile. Nevertheless, gravel and sand are our basic materiality. They are among the most abundant, human-scaled, and easy-to-work "stuff" available on the planet. Because of these properties, however, making something of gravel or sand is rarely regarded as "difficult" in the same way constructing monuments like the pyramids of ancient Egypt or Central America is. Fabrication requiring the mobilization of vast quantities of material substance, human labor, and technological ingenuity is generally regarded as significant, even meaningful, *ipso facto*. In contrast, it is perfectly obvious how things of gravel and sand are made. There is no mystery, no awe surrounding their realization, and, as a consequence, often little regard for their significance or meaning save by those who savor the fleeting and indeterminate.

Although sand and gravel gardens are physically fragile, they have proven extremely strong in terms of the human intention to maintain them against challenges by Nature and the capriciousness of human character.[7] Nevertheless, it would be most peculiar if gravel or sand were used to create enduring legacies if these gardens were not of the ontological category of things that must exist as both new and old simultaneously. Every re-raking, every re-forming, makes a gravel or sand garden anew, yet not really different from how it was before.[8] As with the reprinting of this very book, with each remanufacturing—fresh ink, fresh paper—the book is still, in the most essential way—word for word, picture for picture—the same book. In truth, without the constant remaking—re-forming, re-raking—gardens of gravel and sand would quickly lose their identity to the wind, the rain, earthquakes, gravity, moss, weeds, fallen leaves, and defiant humans. The gardens would *then* fundamentally change, grow old, and disappear.

Some people have confused the foregoing paradoxes, together with the abstract visual composition and extreme simplicity of the gardens—plus the contradiction of water being represented by its manifest material opposite—with core principles of Zen.[9] True, many of the gardens are managed by, and located on the sanctuary-like grounds of, Zen temples. But there is scant historical evidence to support a direct religious or philosophical connection between gardens of gravel and sand—even with some rocks thrown in—and Zen.[10] In fact, the "Zen garden" interpretation shows up for the first time in 1935, in an English-language book titled *One Hundred Kyoto Gardens*.[11] It is not until after the Second World War, in the 1950s, that the concept of gardens of gravel or sand and their surroundings as an expression of Zen even appears in the Japanese language, and then mainly as applied to the garden at the temple Ryoan-ji.[12]

If there is "Zen" in these gardens, it wasn't put there by the people who originally designed and assembled them. The gardens are not the result of mystical insights or spontaneous action like those associated with the Zen "arts" of ink painting, archery, tea ceremony, and so forth. Garden design requires planning and an extended period of time for construction. It is unlikely that any "flash of insight" is involved, or that the gardens are meant to inspire such. Many of these gardens were not even designed or constructed by Zen practitioners at all but by gardeners/garden designers who were of the lowest social class; there is nothing Zen-like or "spiritual" about them.[13]

Possibly art

Why go all the way to Kyoto, you may ask, when you can replicate a garden of gravel or sand from photographs in your backyard, or some similarly enclosed area? Some people have done just that. I have childhood memories of Japanese restaurants in Los Angeles with outdoor patches of raked sand embellished with a few rocks here and there. And I've seen pictures in fashion magazines of a health spa in Southern California with similar arrangements.[14] There are undoubtedly many others.

Assuming that the imitations look exactly like the originals in Kyoto, with the same qualities of maintenance and design nuance—which is unlikely—there are important ways in which they differ. What immediately comes to mind is the setting, the context. A pushpin on the wall of a supermarket bulletin board has a completely different meaning from a similar-looking pushpin on the wall of an art gallery. The specific context within which an experience occurs informs the experience. The context for the Kyoto gardens of gravel and sand is complex, multilayered, and coherent. You are reminded at least six times that you are in the vicinity of the unusual, the well thought out, and the artistic. As you approach the large gravel garden at Daisen-in, for example (photographs on pages 10–15), you encounter in the following order:

(1) Kyoto itself, a slow-paced city with an abundance of beautiful places and things of a refined, detail-intensive, historically referential nature.

(2) The temple precinct, a buffer zone around the temple complex proper. A concentration of shops, restaurants, and other businesses oriented to the tastes and needs of the residents of, and visitors to, the nearby temples.

(3) The main entrance to the Daitoku-ji temple complex, a formal break with the outside world and its concerns. Daisen-in is one of the dozen or so sub-temples within this complex.

(4) The meandering stone and gravel pathways through the Daitoku-ji complex to the Daisen-in grounds.

(5) The entrance to the Daisen-in temple building where the garden is housed. Shoes are taken off here.

(6) A walk along dark wood floors, through a dark interior, to a garden-viewing veranda where you sit or stand to look out onto the courtyard garden, open to the sky, flooded with light.

And (7) perhaps a sonic background of birds chirping, or possibly a priest or monks chanting to the accompaniment of gong, drum beats, and/or bell ringing.[15]

Another significant difference between the original gardens and the imitations is the manner in which each came into existence. The originals were created by people who had internalized the pertinent historical and topical body of knowledge pertaining to garden theory and visual presentation. They were intent on doing something original yet consonant with the current aesthetic and cultural matrix. The imitations have a much thinner creative and cultural grounding. They are more like instant appropriations, not dissimilar from scaled reproductions of, say, the Eiffel Tower or the Piazza San Marco in front of Las Vegas hotels. They are borrowing the iconic aspects of gravel and sand gardens, then adding trendy connotations that have little to do with the orignals.[16]

This is not to imply that all the gardens of gravel and sand in this book are, therefore, site-specific works of art. At least one garden is in actuality a staging area for the practice of magic. The sand cone with a branch sticking out of its top (photographs on pages 34–37), located at a small neighborhood Shinto shrine, is a magical device to call and attract "god spirits."[17] This is *not* art.[18] Nor are the similar-looking cones and environs pictured on pages 10–17. These are piles of symbolically pure gravel waiting to be ceremoniously spread on the ground in the path of visiting dignitaries.[19] The 2-meter-high cone with the flattened top as seen on pages 44–45 and 50–51 is, though, probably art. It is designed as a representation of a volcano, not unlike Mt. Fuji, according to one plausible historical interpretation.[20] (The point is that in all of the extant interpretations of this cone, something more than merely a cone of sand is represented in the manner in which we have come to understand that artworks represent something more than merely themselves.)[21] All of these cones, however, *look* like late-20th-century museum-certified art with their minimalist compositions and minimal use of minimal materials. In an oddly recursive twist, these cones, and most of the other gardens of gravel and sand in this book, seem so much like contemporary art because they have, in many ways, been an inspiration for it. They are at the beginning of a now orthodox lineage of austerely reductive constructions fashioned out of primal materials. When the earliest gardens of gravel and sand were first conceived, however, a Japanese concept of "art," especially as we understand the term today, did not exist.[22]

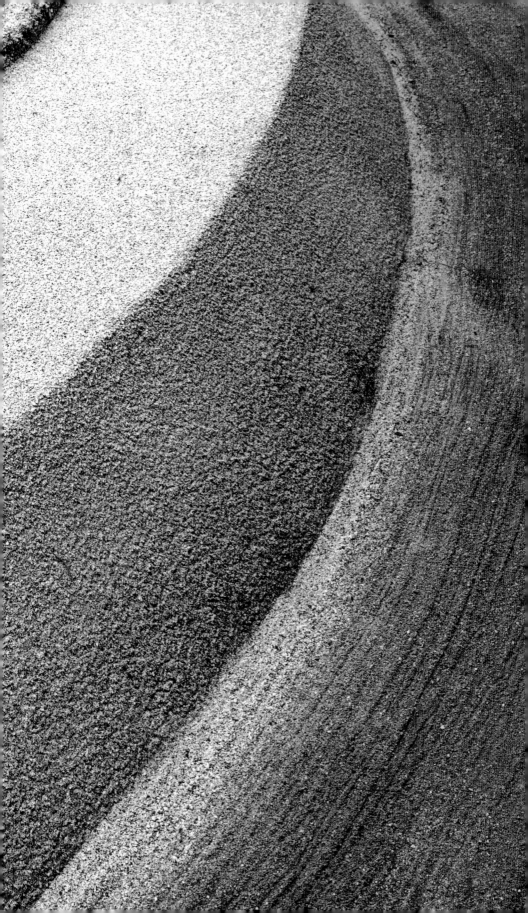

Meta-gardens

According to at least one thoughtful designer of traditional
Japanese-style gardens, the meaning of a garden lies in its sensory
effects and beauty.[23] Alternatively stated, gardens are better experienced than explained. This is the antithesis of contemporary art
appreciation where the explanation, the intellectual buttressing
and precise placement into an art historical context, is absolutely
essential for an "accurate" perception of the artwork.[24] Gardens
of gravel or sand can be experienced within the mental set of
either domain—art or garden—or they can be scrutinized in the
light of religion, Japanese history, and so on. But since there is so
little credible critical discussion or solid (non-revisionist) historical
information pertaining to the gravel and sand gardens, experienc-
ing the garden *as* garden is probably the best way to minimize
intellectual frustration.[25]

Obviously gardens of gravel and sand are not exactly the same
as gardens made up predominately of living things, but they
spring from a similar impulse: to use discrete elements of Nature
in a manner superior—more metaphorically satisfying—to
Nature, albeit on a smaller, more idealized scale. If you are
inclined to wax philosophic, you can say that gardens of gravel
or sand are a kind of "meta-garden." "Meta" is used here in the
sense of "beyond"; meta-gardens exemplify the ultimate concep-

tual refinement of a particular garden type. On a more mundane level, gardens of gravel and sand can be compared to wintertime versions of living gardens when the foliated "flesh" is removed, revealing skeletal, stripped-down forms.

But no matter how you characterize them, gardens of gravel and sand differ from living gardens in at least the following ways:

• In a garden of gravel or sand there is no use for plant prejudices, likes, or dislikes.

• Gardens of gravel and sand change imperceptibly with the seasons; therefore none of the typical life-affirming garden metaphors tied to the seasons—ways of viewing growth, death, and rebirth positively—are relevant. Nor are anticipatory reveries, musings, or daydreams of what/how things will grow, fill out, or be planted next season.

• Few useful skills can be gleaned from extensive experience in gravel or sand gardening.

• In a garden of gravel or sand there is no pretense of trying to follow "Nature's template," trying to simulate a "natural" landscape, or "setting Nature in motion."

• In a garden of gravel or sand anything that is not gravel or sand is an unwanted element, a so-called weed.

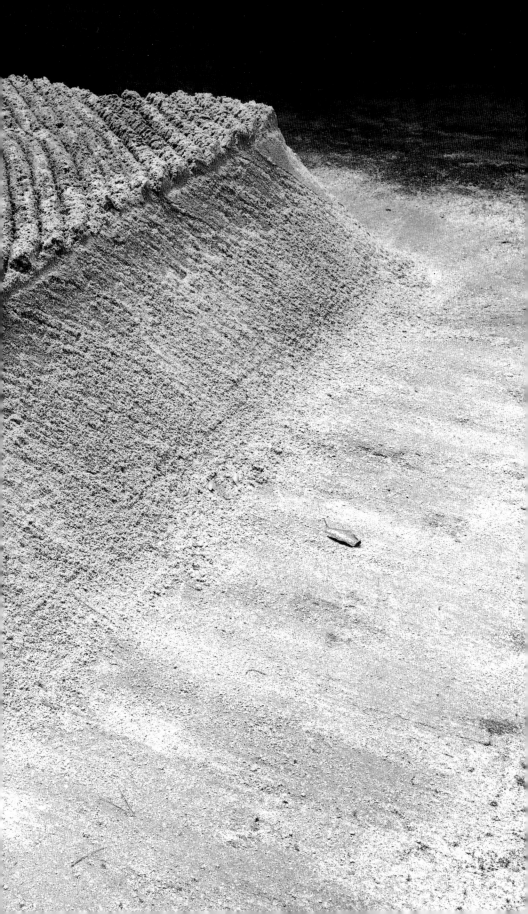

Text notes

1. All of the gravel and sand pictured in this book comes from the granite mountains on the eastern side of Kyoto. The main river flowing out of these mountains, Shirakawa (literally, "White River"), carries down various-sized pieces of the granite's constituents: feldspar (white), quartz (gray), and mica (black). The resulting gravel and sand occurs in various shades of off-white to medium gray. The sizes of the garden-useful particles vary from 2 millimeters to 2 centimeters in diameter. In non-scientific language, there isn't a definitive point at which sand becomes gravel. For the purposes of this book, from a distance of 2 meters individual gravel chunks are visually distinct whereas sand grains aren't.

2. *Kare-san-sui* literally means "dry mountain water." In these gardens, rocks represent islands, mountains, or other large natural features, and gravel or sand represents bodies of water—rivers, seas—surrounding and abutting these geologic representations. Often non-flowering trees and/or trimmed evergreen shrubs are also included in these garden compositions. According to Japanese art historian Yoshinobu Yoshinaga, as translated in David A. Slawson's book *Secret Teachings in the Art of Japanese Gardens* (1987): "The [*kare-san-sui*] garden is an attempt to represent the innermost essence of water, without actually using

water, and to represent it even more profoundly than would be possible with real water."

3. Gardens of gravel or sand, as defined in this book, are usually sub-sections of larger gardens. Omitting all garden elements except the gravel or sand is not simply a rhetorical, dialectical, or interpretive device, however. In some gardens, distinctly segregated sections of gravel or sand have come into their own. Gardens illustrated in this book that fall into this category include Daisen-in (photographs on pages 10–15), Ginkaku-ji (pages 44–51), and Kaizan-do at Tofuku-ji (pages 88–95).

4. "Nature" is defined in this book as the actions of the world without the intrusion of humankind.

5. Figure and ground are actually dependent upon one another like *yin* and *yang*. They work in tandem, one not superior or inferior to the other.

6. The precise origins of the *kare-san-sui* form are historically uncertain. We know that gravel or sand was spread on the grounds of palaces and Shinto shrines going back to the beginnings of Japanese recorded history, although mainly as a ritualistically purifying ground cover. The word *kare-san-sui* is mentioned as early as the 11th century in Japanese garden literature. Originally *kare-san-sui* were small parts of larger gardens. By the 16th century they had become a distinct and independent garden type. The inspiration for *kare-san-sui* comes at least partially from Chinese monochromatic ink brush paintings—a three-dimensional representation thereof—and also probably from bonsai and bonseki, small gardens in trays, featuring plants and rocks respectively.

7. On my occasional visits to the Kyoto gardens I have witnessed occurrences like a young woman, trying to impress her friends, clandestinely pressing her barefoot heel deeply into freshly swept sand. And I have seen teenage schoolboys, spurred on by the dares of their classmates, dash across lines of crisply raked sand at the entrance to one of Kyoto's most famous temples. It is almost as if something intrinsic to these delicately shaped gravel or sand constructions tempts us to violate their tenuous order.

8. It doesn't even matter *who* does the re-raking or re-forming. Various people rake or re-form the Kyoto gravel and sand gardens over time, resulting in a kind of communal authorship. (Even your humble author raked the gravel early one morning at Daisen-in, proving that great skill isn't a necessary attribute in a raker.) There are no precise guides or markers, so each raker or re-former remakes the design according to his own individual understanding. Viewed in time lapse, the garden would appear

as a living organism, slowly writhing and changing shape.

9. Gravel and sand are generally interpreted as representing water in the *kare-san-sui* at Zen temples and former samurai residences, but not in the gravel and sand constructions at Shinto shrines or the decorative flourishes like those at the entrance to Ginkaku-ji (photograph on pages 42–43).

10. According to Wybe Kuitert in his extensively researched book *Themes, Scenes, and Taste in the History of Japanese Garden Art* (1988), there is no mention of *kare-san-sui* as expressions of Zen philosophy in any 18th, 19th, or early 20th century Japanese garden literature. The gardens at the temples, like those at samurai residences, were installed to create an "enhanced cultural ambience."

11. The book's American author, Lorraine Kuck, lived in Kyoto from 1932 to 1935, and was a sometime neighbor of Daisetzu Teitaro Suzuki (1870–1966), the famous interpreter and popularizer of Zen. Kuck has noted that she and Suzuki "discussed Zen." In 1934 Suzuki wrote for the first time about Japanese landscape gardening as an expression of the "spirit of Zen." Suzuki, in turn, was influenced by his friend Kitaro Nishida (1870–1945), an eminent Japanese philosopher who couched his discussions of the "Japanese spirit" in terms of Zen to "universalize" them in the face of the ominously growing use of the "Japanese spirit" concept for racist, nationalistic purposes in pre–World War II Japan.

12. The Ryoan-ji garden is unquestionably the most famous and iconographically potent *kare-san-sui* in our collective contemporary world culture (Japan included). Laid out in about 1499, it occupies an area of 330 square meters. It has fifteen rocks placed on a sea of raked gravel with a wabi-sabi-like wall behind, making it look obviously old and historical. Ryoan-ji is not photographically represented in this book because the rocks are clearly the focus of attention and there is moss in the buffer zone between the rocks and the gravel. (Whether or not this was originally intended is uncertain.) Ryoan-ji received little public notice until the 1930s. In the 1960s Japanese artists and writers began writing about Ryoan-ji's "extraordinary abstract qualities." Ryoan-ji is now maintained as a major tourist attraction annually visited by over 700,000 people. Unfortunately, bus loads of boisterous tourists greatly diminish the garden-viewing experience.

13. Many of the garden designers and garden construction workers were landless social outcasts who were only allowed to do "unclean" jobs like handling the dead, constructing roads, and working with the earth.

14. Specifically, the Golden Door Spa in Escondido (near San Diego). It has a few small sand gardens and one large one, which has often appeared in print, approximately 150 square meters, half the size of Ryoan-ji, its stated model.

15. The garden is thus a jewel-like entity in the very center.

16. The Golden Door Spa (see note 14) has had, on occasion, week-long sand-raking classes as a calming, meditative activity. Although raking sand or gravel can indeed be relaxing or contemplative, it is not treated as anything special at Zen temples in Kyoto. Every menial task (called *samu*)—toilet cleaning, ditch digging, garbage collection, sand raking—is seen as an equally good opportunity for Zen practice. Sand raking in Kyoto is devoid of the romantic "spiritual" overtones it often seems to have outside of Japan.

17. The generic Shinto term for a dwelling place of gods/god spirit, like the sand cone with a branch, is *yori shiro*. The tree branch at the top of the sand cone is used like an antenna to attract these spirits. We assume that the people who went to the effort of raking this sand, forming the cone, and putting a branch on the top, believe that it works as it is expressly designed to.

18. John Cage, among others, has defined art as anything that generates aesthetic experience. For the purposes of this brief discussion, we are ignoring this definition because it is too all encompassing, rendering any further definitions of art moot.

19. At one time this *symbolically* pure gravel may have had the same *magical* qualities of purity as that found in the gravel and sand at Shinto shrines. According to archeologist and garden historian Takahiro Naka (in an interview conducted by Gretchen Mittwer as part of the research for this book), it is the white color of the gravel and sand that is the actual purifying agent. Hence it is the whiteness of the cones of salt outside of Japanese restaurants, for example, that effects the entrance purification. But sea sand, salt, and seawater have been used in ways that would indicate that it is the link to the ocean that is key to the magical purification qualities (according to the *Kojiki* and the *Nihon Shoki*, two official Japanese histories, compiled in a.d. 712 and 720 respectively). To further confuse the issue, sand is used as a purifying agent in other, older cultures that have links to Japan. Zoroastrians who lived in China, for example, used sand in their elaborate purifying rituals.

20. According to Mitchell Bring and Jesse Wayembergh in their book *Japanese Gardens: Design and Means* (1981), during the Edo period (1603–1867), when this cone was added to the garden, the conical shape of Mt. Fuji was a popular motif in

Japanese artistic representations. According to Lorraine Kuck in her book *The World of the Japanese Garden: From Chinese Origins to Modern Landscape Art* (1968), the cone originally could have been just a pile of extra sand, like at Daisen-in (photographs on pages 10–15) or the Hojo of Myoshin-ji (photograph on pages 16–17), used to renew the paths in preparation for visiting dignitaries until it evolved into an aesthetic object. Or, as other interpreters have suggested, the cone could be a moon-reflecting mound or plateau.

21. Implicit in this interpretation is a conscious agreement to *not* perceive the sand cone as simply a cone of sand, but as something else. In a similar manner the oft-quoted Marcel Duchamp artwork titled "Fountain," supposedly an off-the-shelf white porcelain urinal, is regarded as a comment on what is, and what is not, art, and not merely as a common urinal. Of course "Fountain" has such meaning only if viewed within the context of Western art history up to the point in time when it was first exhibited.

22. The opening of Japan to the West in the mid-1800s also brought in Western concepts of art. Though every new period of history sees new things in what was made by previous eras—new perceptual features seem to reveal themselves—the whole range of

metaphors and references that were embedded in these gardens originally is no longer accessible to us. The few historically grounded references available to us—Chinese ink painting (see note 6), gravel or sand as water (see note 2), and so on—are too limited, sentimental, and cliche-ridden today to rely on for sustained enjoyment.

23. According to David A. Slawson, a garden designer and teacher who apprenticed for two years under a Kyoto garden master, designed ten public and twenty private Japanese-style gardens, and wrote the insightful book mentioned in note 2.

24. Look at how almost every contemporary museum catalog tries to provide a critical context for the artwork under review including the minutiae of the artist's prior work (exhibits, names and residences of owners of the artist's work, bibliography of monographs, articles and books about the artist's work, etc.). The viewer is hardly allowed to confront a new work free of canonical preconceptions.

25. Gardens of gravel and sand actually straddle a nonexistent territory between art and gardening: less cant than art but more intellect than typically associated with gardening.

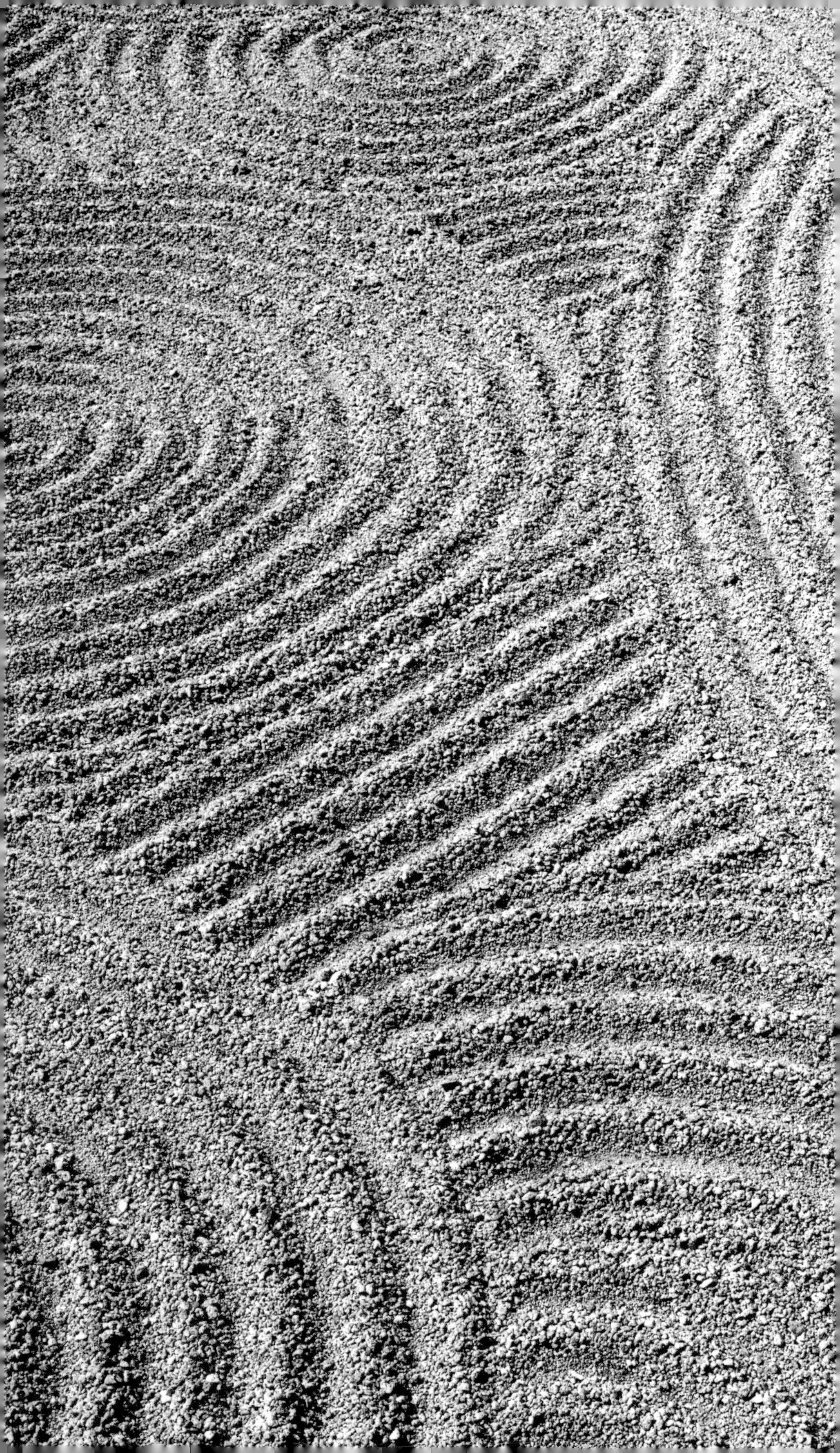

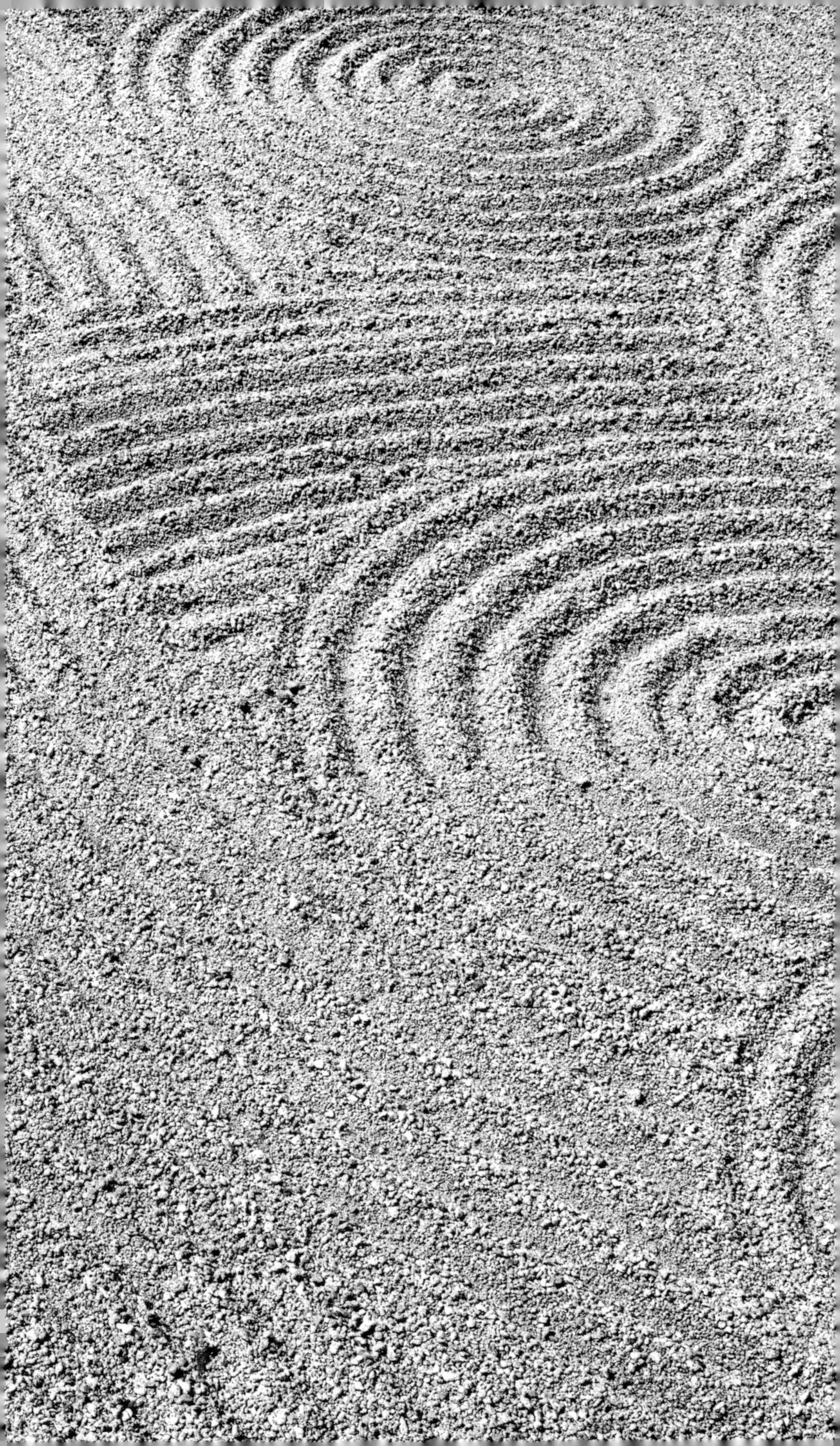

Photograph captions

COVERS—Detail of the large south garden at the Hojo (Abbot's Hall) of Tofuku-ji.

PAGES 4–5—A small gravel garden in front of Korin-in, a sub-temple of Daitoku-ji.

PAGES 6–7—At Shisen-do, one of Japan's first privately developed gardens (established in 1641 by a retired samurai but now the property of the Soto sect of Zen Buddhism), the sand is swept daily with a broom that leaves faint, delicate markings. Most gravel and sand gardens, according to garden custodians, are raked, swept, or re-formed "only when they need it." This basically means after a heavy rain, wind storm, and the like, when the gravel or sand begins to look noticeably ragged.

PAGES 10–15—The head priest of Daisen-in demonstrating proper technique with a heavy metal rake for the author of this book. Note the straw sandals donned especially for raking (you can feel the individual chunks of gravel underfoot). Also note the two ceremonial gravel cones, piled to the angle of repose, waiting to be spread out to form a path for important visiting personages such as a new temple abbot, or the emperor.

PAGES 16–17—Two piles of gravel at the Hojo (Abbot's Hall) of Myoshin-ji. These piles serve the same purpose as at Daisen-in (see above caption). The whole courtyard is supposed to be covered with white gravel, but so much time has elapsed since the last re-graveling that small plants and bare spots of soil are visible. Beautiful in this semi-neglected state, the garden gives a visitor the feeling that the less-than-scrupulous maintenance regime here is possibly intentional.

PAGES 20–23—At Zuiho-in, a sub-temple of Daitoku-ji, deep furrows of various-sized rough gravel—never used quite in this highly expressionistic manner prior to World War II—are designed to impart a sense of turbulent water. This garden was created by Mirei Shigemori (1896–1975) in 1961. Shigemori, a kind of traditional Japanese culture Renaissance man, designed over a hundred gardens and wrote one encyclopedia of Japanese garden history and another encyclopedia of Japanese tea ceremony. He also experimented with the form of the tea ceremony and formulated much of the theory behind current avant-garde styles of *ikebana* (flower arranging).

85

PAGES 24–29—At impeccably manicured Manshu-in, dried moss and mud border the finely raked gravel mounds. As at many *kare-san-sui* (see text note 2), viewing is possible only from a veranda running along one side of the garden.

PAGES 33–37—A sand garden in front of a small Shinto shrine in the vicinity of Manshu-in. Note the cone with tree branch (and attached rice paper) that acts as an antenna to attract god spirits.

PAGES 42–43—This decoratively raked sand treatment at the entrance of Ginkaku-ji is one of the innovations of the current abbot. It is raked often, and differently.

PAGES 44–45—The primary sand garden at Ginkaku-ji was constructed in the 18th century. The sand dais in the foreground is called the "Silver Sea." The sand cone in the distance is supposed to be a representation of one of the sacred volcanic mountains found throughout Japan, or a moon reflecting platform, or just an attractive pile of sand.

PAGES 46–49—Details of the "Silver Sea" at Ginkaku-ji. The sand is mounded, pressed into place, and then raked.

PAGES 50–51—A close-up of the 2-meter-high sand cone, daily re-formed with wood paddles. Observation of old drawings and photographs shows the size and shape of the cone changing over the years. (It's gotten larger.)

PAGES 54–63—One of the two sand mounds at Honen-in, a Jodo sect Buddhist temple. When the temple was originally established here, having moved from another location, there were five mounds. These two mounds haven't changed much since about 1608. Wood boards and rakes are used to renew the form and create a generally water-related motif on the mound's top. The drawing on the top takes abut two hours and is up to the discretion of the drawer.

PAGES 64–67—The other sand mound at Honen-in. Water is sprinkled on the sand now and again. The mounds are never demolished. Here the dried-out mound will soon be wet down and the fallen sand patted back into the main mass.

PAGES 77–83—The large south garden, one of four designed in 1939 by Mirei Shigemori (see caption for pages 20–23) at the Hojo (Abbot's Hall) of Tofuku-ji.

PAGES 89–95—This rare checkerboard pattern sand garden is at Kaizan-do at Tofuku-ji. Some interpreters say this design represents abstracted horizontal and vertical water ripples. Others suggest that it represents rice fields.

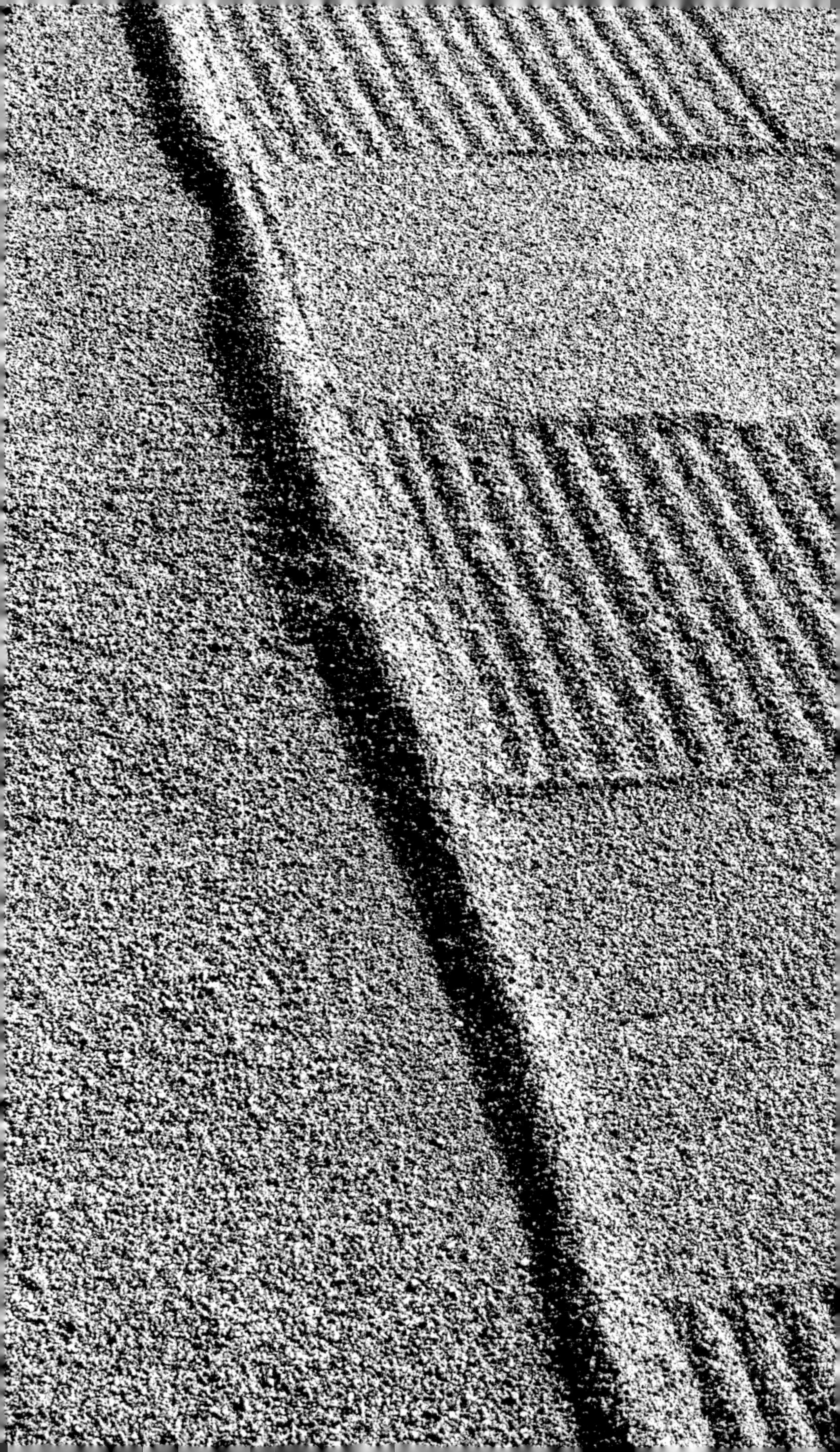

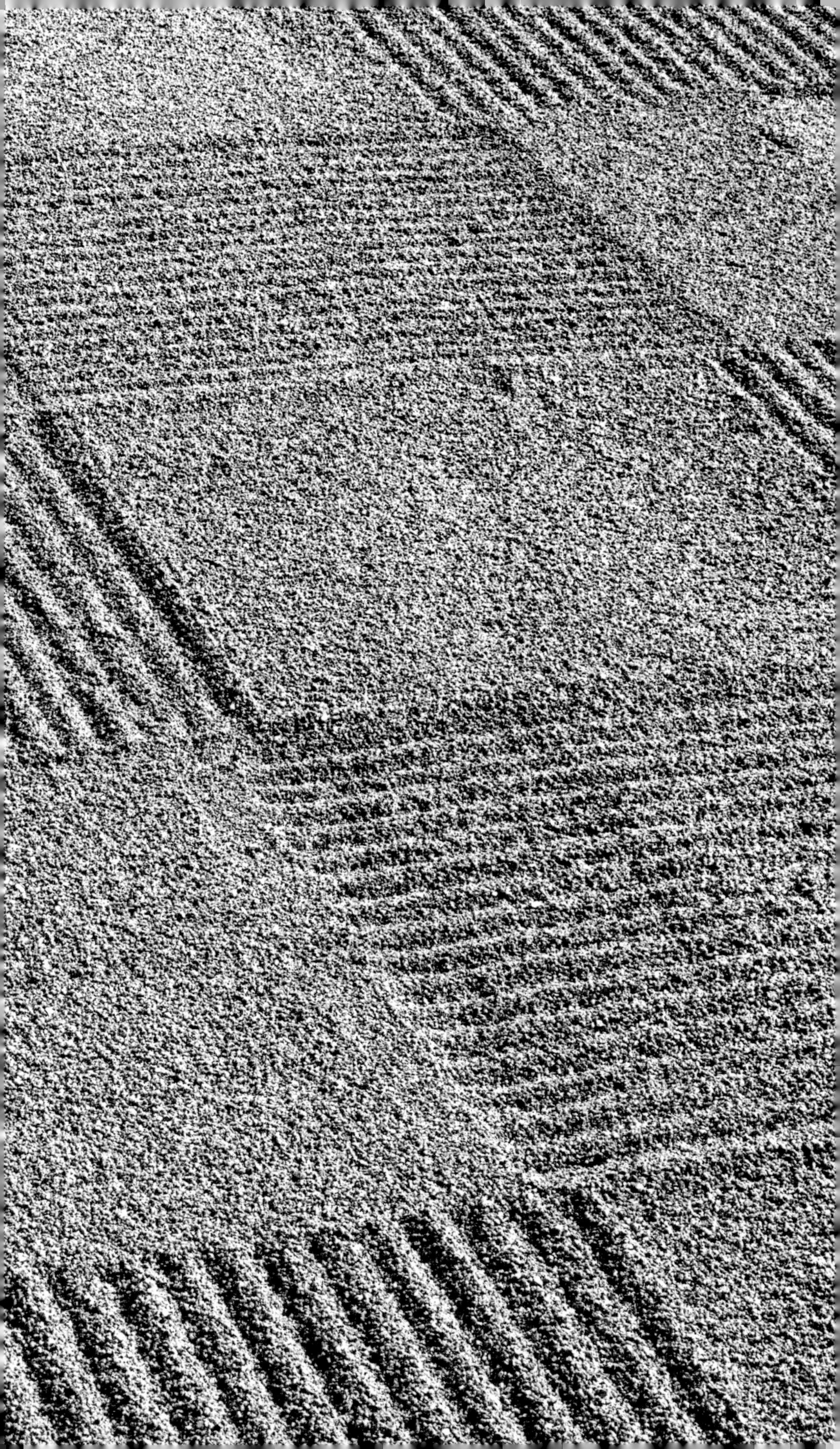